D0962512

COURAGEOUS CANINE!

And More True Stories of Amazing Animal Heroes

Published by the National Geographic Society
John M. Fahey, *Chairman of the Board and Chief Executive Officer*
Declan Moore, *Executive Vice President; President, Publishing and Travel*
Melina Gerosa Bellows, *Executive Vice President; Chief Creative Officer, Books, Kids, and Family*

Prepared by the Book Division
Hector Sierra, *Senior Vice President and General Manager*
Nancy Laties Feresten, *Senior Vice President, Kids Publishing and Media*
Jay Sumner, *Director of Photography, Children's Publishing*
Jennifer Emmett, *Vice President, Editorial Director, Children's Books*
Eva Absher-Schantz, *Design Director, Kids Publishing and Media*
R. Gary Colbert, *Production Director*
Jennifer A. Thornton, *Director of Managing Editorial*

Staff for This Book
Marfé Ferguson Delano, *Project Editor*
Becky Baines, *Editor*
Lisa Jewell, *Illustrations Editor*
David Seager, *Art Director*
Ruthie Thompson, *Designer*
Grace Hill and Michael O'Connor, *Associate Managing Editors*
Joan Gossett, *Production Editor*
Lewis R. Bassford, *Production Manager*
Susan Borke, *Legal and Business Affairs*
Ariane Szu-Tu, *Editorial Assistant*
Callie Broaddus, *Design Production Assistant*
Hillary Moloney, *Illustrations Assistant*

Manufacturing and Quality Management
Phillip L. Schlosser, *Senior Vice President*
Chris Brown, *Vice President, NG Book Manufacturing*
George Bounelis, *Vice President, Production Services*
Nicole Elliott, *Manager*
Rachel Faulise, *Manager*
Robert L. Barr, *Manager*

Table of CONTENTS

LILLY: Courageous Canine   4

    Chapter 1: Love at First Sight   6

    Chapter 2: Lilly to the Rescue   16

    Chapter 3: A New Career   26

DOLPHINS: Daring Rescuers   36

    Chapter 1: Shark Attack!   38

    Chapter 2: A Pod of Protectors   48

    Chapter 3: Life Savers   58

BINTI JUA AND JAMBO:
Gorilla Good Guys   68

    Chapter 1: Boy Meets Gorilla   70

    Chapter 2: Bringing Up Binti   80

    Chapter 3: Another Great Ape   90

DON'T MISS!   101

Index and More Information   110

LILLY:
COURAGEOUS
CANINE

Lilly stands strong on her three legs. Her beautiful golden eyes seem to shine with courage.

Lilly the pit bull is gentle and sweet. She loves to be scratched under her ears.

LOVE at First Sight

For Lilly, it started as an ordinary day. The five-year-old dog paced across her cage at the Animal Rescue League (sounds like LEEG) in Boston, Massachusetts. She ate her breakfast kibble. She curled up on her blanket to take short naps. Once in a while, she even barked with the other dogs. But she mostly seemed sad and lonely. Like the rest of the animals at the shelter, she needed a home.

That March morning in 2009 started out as a regular day for David Lanteigne (sounds like LAN-tane), too. But he was excited. He was going to do something new later that day. Something awesome.

He was going to volunteer at the Animal Rescue League (ARL).

David is a police officer in Boston. He works five days a week helping people. On his day off, he wanted to help homeless dogs. At the shelter, David filled out the forms to become a volunteer. Then he asked if he could meet the canines (sounds

Did You Know?

Puppies have 28 baby teeth. They start to lose them at around four months old. Then adult teeth grow in— about 42 of them.

like KAY-nines). He meant the dogs.
Dogs belong to the group of animals
called canines.

"Sure," the ARL workers said.
"Come this way."

Slowly, David strolled past the cages.
He felt good about the job he had signed
up to do. All of the dogs needed loving
care, and he was just the guy to deliver it.
Then, six cages in, his heart skipped a
beat. He was face-to-face with Lilly.

"Hello, sweet girl," he said. Lilly's
golden eyes met his. "You have the most
beautiful eyes in the world," David told her.

Lilly calmly walked to the edge of her
cage where David waited. He gazed into
her gentle eyes. Then he noticed deep scars
on the dog's left side. There were scars on

the top of her head, too. *Lilly has been mistreated,* David thought. *What kind of person could hurt such a warm-hearted dog?*

Lilly pressed her soft brown body against her cage to get closer to David. He felt like she was telling him, *I have been hurt, but I still know how to be good.*

David sat down beside the cage to talk to Lilly. "You *are* a good girl," he whispered. He stroked her fur through the cage. She liked it when he scratched her under her chin and behind her floppy ears. Her personality sparkled like a diamond.

"Can I walk one of the dogs?" David asked an ARL worker. "I think Lilly would like to go outside."

Lilly loved walking with David. They galloped through the grass and down the streets. She gave David dozens of sloppy licks. For man and dog, it was love at first sight. David realized he didn't just want to walk Lilly. He wanted to take her home.

To adopt Lilly, David needed to know if another dog and another person would love her, too. He had to introduce her to his dog, Penny. She's a golden retriever (sounds like ree-TREE-ver). David also wanted Lilly to meet his mom, Christine. David hoped Christine would share Lilly with him. He knew his mom got sad and lonely at times. He hoped taking care of Lilly would make her feel happier.

David drove to his mother's house. She lived about an hour away, in Shirley, Massachusetts. David told her about Lilly.

"Just meet her," he said. "Then you can decide if you like her as much as I do." Christine agreed to go meet Lilly.

Like David, Christine thought Lilly was beautiful. She was a little scared about walking her, though. Lilly is an American pit bull terrier (sounds like TER-ee-er), or pit bull for short. She weighs 70 pounds (32 kg). When she tugged at the leash, Christine could feel how strong she was. But Lilly seemed to understand Christine's fear. She quickly settled down.

Before they took Lilly back inside the shelter, David went to his car. Penny's dog biscuits were in the trunk. He wanted to share them with Lilly. When he popped the trunk open, Lilly jumped inside. She was ready to go home!

What are pit bulls?

The first pit bulls
were probably a
cross between two kinds
of dogs: the English bulldog
and the Old English terrier. People
in England created the breed about
200 years ago. The dogs were strong,
smart, and loyal. They made excellent
hunting and watch dogs. In America,
farmers used pit bulls to help protect
cattle and sheep from wild animals.
In the early 1900s, some pit bulls even
looked after children. This earned them a
special nickname. They were called
"nanny dogs."

A few days later, David took Penny to the shelter to meet Lilly. The two dogs got along very well. "That was it," David says. "No matter what, I knew we were adopting Lilly."

David and his mom shared Lilly, but the dog spent most of her time at Christine's house in Shirley. Some people told Christine she should be afraid of keeping a pit bull in her home. They thought all pit bulls were dangerous. They thought the dogs liked to attack people. Christine didn't listen to them. She trusted her son.

David knew the dogs weren't born bad. But some cruel owners force their pit bulls to fight other dogs. These fights are against the law. Sometimes the dogs are badly hurt. Sometimes it's even worse. All of this made David sad.

Being forced to fight can make an animal mean, but kindness can sometimes make it better. Christine believed David when he said Lilly was a loving dog, and he was right. Lilly kept her company when she got lonely. In return, Christine cooked Lilly yummy meals. They went on lots of walks together. Lilly made many new friends as she and Christine walked through town.

Thanks to David and Christine, Lilly had a safe place to live. She had plenty of good food to eat. Best of all, she got lots and lots of love. David and his mom had given her a second chance at life. One day Lilly would return the favor.

Lilly (top) and Penny (bottom) both like to hang out at the park. They've been friends ever since they met.

Chapter 2

LILLY to the RESCUE

Lilly the gentle pit bull and Christine lived a happy life together. David and Penny visited often to play. Sometimes Lilly and Christine went to Boston to see them. The police officer was proud of how his mother cared for Lilly. Then in May 2012, disaster struck.

One night Christine had trouble getting to sleep. So she decided to take Lilly for a late-night stroll. Together, they walked across the railroad tracks near their home.

They had crossed the tracks a thousand times before. But something went wrong that night. Christine suddenly felt dizzy. Lilly stood by her as she wobbled and fell. Then Christine blacked out. She didn't see the bright light shining in the distance, but Lilly did. A freight train was rocketing their way.

The daring dog sprang into action. Lilly barked an urgent warning. Christine did not wake up. Lilly nipped and snapped at her owner's arms and legs. Still nothing, as danger thundered on. Frantic, Lilly began to tug at Christine's clothes. The train drew closer and closer.

Finally, the train engineer saw the dog and woman on the tracks. He tried to stop the heavy train, but it was going too fast. In the nick of time, Lilly dragged Christine off the tracks. Then the dog wrapped her body around the woman. The train hurtled by. The engineer felt a thump.

When the train rolled to a stop, he jumped to the ground. In a panic, he ran back to Lilly and Christine. He knew the train had hit something. "I thought they were dead," he later said. They were not. In fact, Christine didn't have a scratch on her. Lilly was not so lucky.

The engineer called for help. He looked down at the heroic pit bull. Her front right leg was covered in blood. It was badly hurt. She seemed unable to stand. But her golden eyes shined with courage. To his amazement, she was alert and friendly. She was also determined to stay close to Christine.

Police officers, firefighters, and paramedics (sounds like pare-uh-MED-iks) rushed to the scene of the accident. They phoned David. They told him his mother was all right, but Lilly was hurt. David had just started his evening shift in Boston. His boss knew how much he loved Lilly, though. "Go!" he told him. In a flash, David was on his way.

The paramedics wrapped Lilly's injured leg in bandages. They tried to calm her.

Many wounded dogs try to bite people who come near them. Lilly did not. So the paramedics petted and comforted her. They spoke to her softly. "It will be okay, girl," they said. "Help is on the way."

Animal control officers soon arrived to help Lilly. They wrapped her in a blanket and drove her to an emergency clinic for pets. But Lilly's wounds were too serious for the clinic staff to fix. The train had nearly torn her right paw off. It was very, very bad. All the clinic doctors could do was wait for David. They knew he would have some hard choices to make.

When David pulled up to the animal clinic, he was afraid. He knew his mother was safe. *But how badly hurt was Lilly? Would anyone be able to help her? Would she survive?* Tears filled his eyes, just thinking about it. He blinked them away. He needed to focus on helping his dog.

"What should I do?" David asked the clinic doctors. But Lilly was the one that answered. When she heard David's voice, she turned to look at him. She softly wagged her tail. Lilly wasn't giving up. So David wouldn't either.

"I saw the same beautiful eyes I saw when I adopted her," David says. "I felt the same bond."

The clinic doctors suggested David take Lilly to Angell (sounds like ANE-juhl) Animal Medical Center in Boston. They told him it was the best animal hospital in the state. If the doctors there couldn't help Lilly, no one could.

Famous Pit Bulls

FOR THE RED, WHITE & BLUE
TRUE BLUE—
THRU AND THRU
ME & YOU

- In 1904, the Buster Brown company used a pit bull named Tige to sell shoes.

- During World War I (1914–1918), the pit bull was used to represent America on posters and postcards.

- In the 1920s, a series of short movies called "Our Gang" featured a sweet pit bull. It had a black ring around its eye and was named Pansy. Later the movies were renamed "The Little Rascals." Pansy also got a new name—Petey.

Gently, David lifted the dog's broken body. He carried her to his car. He put her on a soft, clean blanket. "Dad's here," he whispered. "Everything is going to be okay."

The 45-minute drive to the animal hospital seemed to take forever. David spoke softly to Lilly most of the way. "Hang on, girl," he told her. "We'll be there soon." When he wasn't talking to Lilly, he fought back tears. He just wanted her to be all right.

Angell doctors were waiting in the emergency room when David carried Lilly in. They scrambled to save her. They quickly eased her pain with medicine and x-rayed her paw. Then they told David that Lilly needed an operation, or surgery (sounds like SIR-juhr-ee). It would be very expensive. David didn't care. "Anything for Lilly," he said. Then he kissed the dog's head.

When the surgery started, David drove home for a shower and a change of clothes. As he toweled off his hair, the phone rang. It was the hospital. Lilly's injuries were far worse than they had first thought. Her hips were broken in several places. Her right leg would have to be removed. The price for the operation soared. It would cost more than ten thousand dollars.

David didn't think twice about the cost. Brave, beautiful Lilly had saved his mother's life. "Do it," he said. "We'll find a way to make it work."

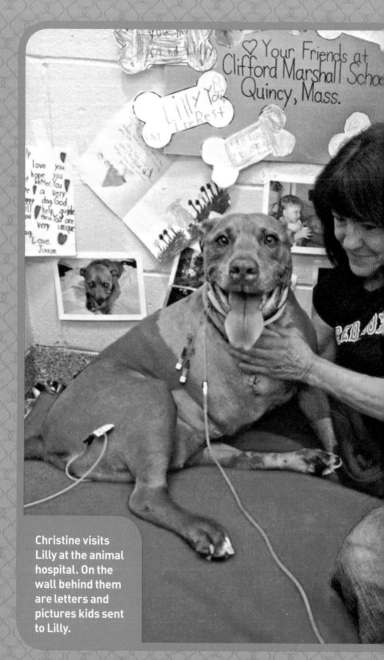

Christine visits Lilly at the animal hospital. On the wall behind them are letters and pictures kids sent to Lilly.

Chapter 3

A NEW CAREER

Poor Lilly. She was quite a sight after her surgery. Her body was covered in stitches. Tubes stuck out here and there. "She looked like Frankenstein's monster," David said. The doctors had shaved off Lilly's fur. David could see dozens of bruises on her skin. But she still licked and nuzzled him and her caregivers at the hospital.

Lilly's loving spirit was still strong, even when her body wasn't.

Lilly was tough, too. She hung in there. So did David. But the medical bills were stacking up. He started to worry.

Then came some good luck. The people at the Angell center fell in love with Lilly. They were amazed at how hard she worked to get better. They offered to pay half her medical bills. Word of this began to get around. Newspapers ran stories about the courageous (sounds like cuh-RAY-jus) canine. TV stations sent camera crews. Then kindness spread like wildfire. Lilly's story touched people everywhere. They sent money to help pay her bills. In four days, the center received $76,000!

The Angell center was thrilled. It agreed to cover all of Lilly's medical bills— for life! The rest of the money would go to other animals in need. Lilly's courage had saved David's mother. Now her story would help save other injured animals.

Lilly became a star. Fans sent her dog cookies and stuffed animals. She got "get well" cards and even a fancy "get well" collar. Kids drew pictures and mailed them to her. Dog owners sent her pictures of their own dogs. Soon, hundreds of photos and cards covered Lilly's room at the hospital.

When she was well enough, Lilly started physical therapy (sounds like

FIZ-uh-kul THER-uh-pee). People in physical therapy do special exercises to help them get better. So how did Lilly do physical therapy? On a special doggy treadmill—in the water! First, the therapist put her into a special harness, or set of straps. This kept Lilly afloat, kind of like a life jacket. Then Lilly did a three-legged walk on the treadmill. This helped her build up the muscles (sounds like MUS-uhls) in her legs and hips.

The treadmill worked. Lilly's muscles got stronger. Next, it was time to try swimming. Again, the therapist strapped her into the special harness. Then Lilly paddled around the pool. Little by little, day by day, she grew stronger.

Finally, the doctors decided Lilly was well enough to go home. Hooray! But she still had a lot of healing to do. David and Christine would have to help her a lot. They would have to keep her from trying to walk or run too soon. And they would have to take her to physical therapy every week.

Christine was fine now. But she was heartbroken by what Lilly had been through. She thought it would be best if the dog stayed at David's house. She still saw Lilly almost every day, though. The brave dog had helped her when she needed it most. Now it was Christine's turn. When David went to work, Christine stayed with Lilly. When he worked late at night, she slept by Lilly's side.

Wild Relatives

The dogs we keep as pets or working animals are called domestic dogs. No matter what their size or shape, all domestic dogs are the same species (sounds like SPEE-sheez), or kind, of dog. The other 35 species of the dog family are a wild bunch. Really! They're called wild dogs, and they include wolves, foxes, and coyotes. Jackals and dingoes are also wild dogs. The smallest wild dog is a tiny fox called a fennec (sounds like FIH-nick), shown here. It weighs about 2 to 3 pounds (1 to 1.5 kg).

Together, David and Christine made sure the dog was never alone. With their loving care, Lilly learned to walk again. She only had three legs, but that was enough!

One day David took Lilly to the park. They came across some elderly women who were enjoying the sun. At first, the women were afraid of Lilly. They thought pit bulls were attack dogs. Then they noticed Lilly's missing leg. They began talking with David. He told them Lilly's story. They began petting the gentle dog. They saw how sweet she was.

"Those five ladies changed their minds," David says. That got him thinking. *Lilly made the women in the park rethink their fear of pit bulls. Could she change other minds?* Turns out, the answer was yes.

Today, Lilly still goes to physical therapy once a week. But that's not all. "People want to meet Lilly," David says. The invitations roll in. She gets invited to schools, senior citizen centers, and more. David takes her as often as he can.

"We are changing how people think about pit bulls," David says. "They do have a bad rap right now. But look at Lilly. Even after what she's been through, she is loving and caring. She's a super-friendly dog. She shows the true nature of the pit bull."

Volunteers helped David create a special group to help more dogs. It's called the "Lilly the Hero Pit Bull" Fund. They sell

T-shirts and stickers at Lilly's special events to raise money. That money helps pay for food and shelter for homeless pit bulls. It also helps provide medical care for wounded pit bulls.

David hopes that in the future Lilly can do even more good. Perhaps she can visit injured soldiers or kids who have been badly hurt. David hopes she can help them feel they are not alone in their struggle to get well. If she can live a good life with three legs, maybe they'll feel hopeful, too.

No matter what the future holds, Lilly is happy to be alive. She gobbles her dinner and enjoys a treat now and then. She runs and plays like other dogs, even with one leg missing. Best of all, she has people who love her. Just as she loves them!

Bottlenose dolphins are fast, strong, curious, and clever. Some are also heroic.

DOLPHINS: DARING RESCUERS

Surfer Todd Endris catches a ride on an ocean wave.

Chapter 1

SHARK Attack!

Imagine if you could go surfing every day! Todd Endris does. He lives near the beach in Marina (sounds like ma-REE-nuh), California. Todd started surfing when he was 16 years old and fell in love with the sport. He almost never misses a day on the water. But on the morning of August 28, 2007, his surfing days nearly came to an end. So did his life.

It was his father's birthday. Todd was taking the day off from work. He planned to go to his dad's party. But he had a little time before it started. He decided to hit the waves at Marina State Beach.

Todd put on his wet suit. The close-fitting rubber suit would help him stay warm in the chilly ocean waters. Then he drove to the beach. It was about 11:30 when he entered the water and paddled out to play.

Marina State Beach is a special place. It is part of the Monterey (sounds like mon-tuh-RAY) Bay National Marine Sanctuary (sounds like SANK-choo-air-ee). The sanctuary stretches along 276 miles (444 km) of coastline from San Francisco to Big Sur, California.

The sanctuary teems with wildlife. It's home to dolphins and whales and many other marine mammals. There are more seabirds than you can shake a feather at: 94 different kinds! There are clams and crabs, and 345 different kinds of fish. Some of these animals are prey (sounds like PRAY). That means they are hunted and eaten by other animals. The animals that do the hunting and eating are called predators (sounds like PRED-uh-ters).

Todd's favorite stretch of the sanctuary included the area nicknamed the "Red Triangle." It's known as the home base for one of the deadliest predators in the sea— the great white shark. Shark attacks happen, and Todd knew it. He also knew they are very, very rare. Between 1959 and

2007, only 50 people in the whole world had been hurt by great whites. That's about one attack a year. Attacks usually happened between late August and November. That's when great whites get hungry for seals.

"It's always in the back of your mind," Todd admits. "You know they are out there." And it was late August. Todd decided to surf anyway.

The tall, blond man paddled out on his six-foot (1.8 m) surfboard and caught a wave. Playful bottlenose dolphins swam through the ocean waters beside him. *Outstanding,* Todd thought, as he rode a wave to shore. He paddled back out to catch another wave. The dolphins went with him.

Shark Snacks

The great white shark in the movie *Jaws* loved to attack and eat people. In reality, sharks rarely dine on humans. They are curious, however. Shark expert A. Peter Klimley says great whites bite things to figure out what they are. "They take a bite, feel them over," he says.

Most great whites release their human victims after a sample bite. People are too bony for their taste. Great whites prefer seals and sea lions, which have thick layers of fat. People are harder to digest.

Some of Todd's human buddies were also surfing. He decided to stop and watch them for a minute. Todd's legs dangled down on either side of his board. He watched his friend Brian Simpson catch a sweet ride. *Awesome,* Todd thought, then . . .

BAM!

Something huge slammed into Todd at 20 miles an hour (32 km/h). It seemed to come out of nowhere. He screamed. Now his friends turned to watch *him.* But they could hardly believe what they saw. An enormous great white shark had rammed Todd hard. He and his surfboard were launched more than 15 feet (4.6 m) into the air. Then the shark waited for him to land.

Rows and rows of sharp, powerful teeth clamped down on Todd's back the instant he hit the water. His surfboard came between his stomach and the shark's bottom teeth. But the giant fish still had Todd's body in its jaws.

The shark began to shake him. Then Todd started the fight of his life. He balled up his fists. He punched the shark again and again. He hoped to hit its eyes, but he had no way of knowing where his fist was landing. Even when he did land a punch, it didn't slow the shark down much. "It was like fighting a car," Todd says.

Blood started to swirl in the splashing water. Todd knew it was his own, but he felt almost no pain. The shark had chomped through many of the nerves in his back. Todd was afraid, but he couldn't give up. "I didn't want to die," he says.

To Todd's surprise, the shark let go! But it was only for a moment. It charged back at Todd. This time it knocked him off his surfboard. Then it opened wide and tried to swallowed Todd's right leg.

Todd started to kick the shark in the face with his left leg. At last, he broke free of the deadly jaws.

Todd knew he needed to swim for the beach. But how could a wounded man escape a shark the size of an SUV? Todd needed a miracle. And that's what he got.

The dolphins started "going absolutely crazy," Todd says. Dolphins leaped out of the water above his head. They darted beneath his bloody leg. They slapped the surface of the water with their flat tails. They even formed a wall with their bodies between Todd and the shark.

Todd's friend Wes Williams saw the whole thing. "At first, I thought, *What did Todd do to make the dolphins mad?*" Wes says. Then he understood. The dolphins were not angry with Todd. They were mad at the shark. The dolphins didn't want to hurt Todd. They wanted to help him.

"Grab your board, Todd!" yelled another friend, Joe Jansen. Joe paddled close. He knew Todd would need help getting to shore. He helped Todd ease his body onto his broken surfboard. Then a soft wave rose and carried them to the safety of the beach.

Dolphins look like they are smiling, but that's just the shape of their mouth.

Chapter 2

A POD OF PROTECTORS

Todd didn't know why the dolphins rescued him from the shark. But one thing is for sure, he's not the only person who owes his life to dolphins. Just ask Rob Howe and his 15-year-old daughter Nicole. Along with two of Nicole's friends, they also escaped disaster, thanks to a pod, or group, of dolphins.

It happened on a beautiful

October day in 2004, at a place called Ocean Beach in New Zealand. Rob and Nicole went there for a swim. Nicole's friends Karina Cooper and Helen Slade joined them. Helen was a bit nervous. She had almost drowned in the bay off Ocean Beach when she was a little girl. She hadn't been back to swim there since. But she was older now. She agreed to give it a try.

Rob, Nicole, and Karina were all trained lifeguards. They were off duty that day. The three of them were also endurance (sounds like in-DUR-ence), or long-distance, swimmers. They also knew special ocean rescue techniques. So Helen was in good hands.

Rob and the three teenagers dove into the crashing waves. They headed for a circle of giant rocks. Inside the circle, the water whirled round and round. The girls loved

jumping into the swirling water. It was like being inside a giant washing machine. As she was tossed and turned, Nicole cut her leg on one of the rocks. But she didn't care. To her and her friends, bloody gashes from the whirlpool were like battle scars.

Next, Rob suggested they go on a training swim. It was half a mile (800 m) across the width of the bay. He knew Helen wasn't a great swimmer. But he and the other two girls had their lifeguard floats with them. If Helen got tired, she could safely rest on the floats along the way. So off they went.

Dolphin Chit-Chat

Bottlenose dolphins sure are noisy. They click. They chirp. They growl. And they whistle. But one whistle may be more important than all the others. One whistle may be a dolphin's very own name. According to scientists, the dolphins develop their name whistle as babies. Then they use it to announce themselves to their family members for the rest of their lives. That means dolphins may be able to talk to each other like people do, rather than just making sounds.

Nicole never even thought about the blood on her leg. She should have. Blood attracts sharks. Great whites can smell blood from a distance of up to three miles (4.8 km) away.

Halfway across the bay, the swimmers stopped to let Helen rest. Helen used the float. The others treaded water. Then something odd happened. A dolphin darted past them. It was so close, they could have touched it. The swimmers were startled, but they swam on. Soon another dolphin joined the first one. The two of them swam with the humans for a few feet. Then the dolphins started "behaving really weird," Rob says.

They started swimming in tight circles around Rob and the girls. The girls cried out, "What's going on? What's happening?" But Rob had no answers. He'd been close to bottlenose dolphins before. More than 500 of them lived in the waters off Ocean Beach. They liked to watch and gently play with human beings. But this was different from anything he'd ever seen. Especially now that more dolphins were showing up.

Soon seven huge dolphins formed a ring around the frightened people. They herded them together, like dogs herd sheep. Closer and closer they pushed them, until the people could hardly move. Were the dolphins trying to hurt them? The girls and Rob knew that dolphins rarely harm humans, but they had to wonder.

Thirty minutes passed. The girls were cold and tired. They couldn't tread water much longer. Rob needed answers. So he forced his way out of the dolphin circle. Helen went with him. Rob hoped he could get a better look at what was happening. What he saw took his breath away.

A huge shadow moved beneath the circle he left behind. A great white shark was stalking them!

Now Rob understood. The dolphins were trying to keep them safe. And Rob had just made it twice as hard. The dolphins now had two groups to protect, instead of one.

Meanwhile, a lifeguard named Matt Fleet watched the group of swimmers from a distance. He thought they were playing with the dolphins. He and another lifeguard cruised closer in their motorized rescue boat. Matt, who knew Rob and the others, decided to join the fun. He dove into the water. Almost at once, he saw the huge shadow. He recognized the danger—

a great white shark! But there was no turning back. So he joined Nicole and Karina inside the dolphin circle.

Did You Know?

Bottlenose dolphins eat fish, shrimp, and squid.

Suddenly, the dolphins got more active. Some still swam in close circles around Matt and the two girls. Some dove under their feet. Some loudly slapped their tails against the top of the water. Rob understood why the dolphins were frantic. So did Matt. But it was too loud to explain to the terrified girls. All that was left to do was wait things out and hope for the best.

Almost as quickly as the commotion started, things began to calm down. The dolphins loosened the circle around Nicole, Karina, and Matt. Most of them eventually swam away. Rob and Helen made their way back to the other swimmers. Luckily for them, the great white shark had swum away. It must have decided not to take on so many large dolphins. It was hungry, but not that hungry!

Matt's co-worker rushed the rescue boat to the swimmers' side. Everyone made it safely to the shore. It had started out as a great day for a swim. Now it still was a great day, thanks to the heroic action of so many brave dolphins.

Todd stands by the patch of sea where dolphins saved him from a shark attack. He still loves to surf.

Chapter 3

LIFE SAVERS

Unlike Rob and Nicole and their friends, Todd Endris was not out of danger once the dolphins saved him. He was badly hurt. The shark had stripped back the skin on his back like a banana peel. Blood gushed from the deep bite to his leg.

Todd's friends rushed to his side. They dragged him onto the beach.

His buddy Brian Simpson knew how to help. He tied his surfboard leash above the bite on Todd's leg. That helped to slow the blood loss. He tried to help his hurt friend calm down. Someone called 911.

A helicopter rushed Todd to the hospital. For the next six hours, doctors pieced Todd back together, like a jigsaw puzzle. The shark's teeth had nearly poked a hole in one of his lungs. Todd was lucky to be alive.

Todd stayed in the hospital for six days. He left with 500 stitches and 200 staples holding him together. A 40-inch (1-m) scar ran down his back.

Todd went to physical therapy (sounds like FIZ-uh-kul THER-uh-pee). He did special exercises there to help his body heal. Day by day he grew stronger. At night, however, Todd battled bad dreams. Nightmares of giant sharks woke him from his sleep. But he also dreamed of dolphins. Those were good dreams.

Six weeks after the shark attack, Todd felt well enough to face his fears. He hopped into his truck. He drove to Marina State Beach. He carried his brand-new surfboard to the water. Then he paddled out to the place where he'd met the shark. "I had to get on with it," he says. "I'm a surfer at heart."

Todd caught a perfect wave. He rode it all the way to the beach. Later he walked back to his truck. On the way, he thought

> **Did You Know?**
>
> **Scientists say bottlenose dolphins can recognize themselves in a mirror.**

about everything that had happened. He thought about how he had fought to recover. He thought about how the shark had just swam away.

In the end, Todd was okay with all that. He had survived. He wasn't angry at the shark. True, it had tried to make a meal of him. But Todd understood the predator was just following its nature. Surfers know some animals in the water can be deadly. He was in the shark's space, Todd says, "not the other way around."

Today life is good for Todd. He runs his own aquarium service company. He got married not too long ago. He still surfs almost every day. And he's helping to create technology to defend surfers against shark attacks.

Click, Click, Click

As a bottlenose dolphin swims, it makes clicking sounds—up to 1,000 of them a second! The clicks travel through the water. When they hit an object like a fish or a rock, the sounds bounce back to the dolphin like an echo. By listening to the echoes, the dolphin can tell the size, shape, and location of the object. This is called echolocation (sounds like ek-oh-loh-CAY-shun). Dolphins use echolocation to find food, avoid enemies, and steer clear of boats.

Todd also speaks out for the brave animals that protected him from the great white shark. He's told his story on TV shows. He's been interviewed by magazines and newspapers. He's talked to dolphin researchers. He supports groups that help protect dolphins. Dolphins are Todd's heroes. He is very grateful to them.

"The dolphins defended me from an animal that was going to kill me," he says. "The shark didn't bite me once. He went for me three times. He wanted to eat me. The dolphins stopped him from doing that."

Why did the dolphins protect Todd and the swimmers in New Zealand? It may have been a friendly habit. Dolphins are very social animals. They live in groups called pods. The mothers nurse and protect their babies, called calves, for up to eight years. In fact, all dolphins in a pod look out for each other.

Dolphins have been known to come to the aid of a sick or hurt dolphin. Like all mammals, dolphins breathe air. They go to the water's surface two or three times a minute to take a breath through the blowhole on top of their head. Often a hurt dolphin has trouble swimming up to breathe. Other dolphins may support it with their flippers and help it to the surface.

Scientist Richard Connor of the University of Massachusetts studies dolphin behavior. He says they have emotions like humans do. When dolphins are happy, he says, they "pet and stroke each other in a very gentle way." He also says, "It's easy to tell when they are upset with each other." Dolphins don't show anger on their faces, like humans do. But they do make sounds that signal they are mad.

Scientists say dolphins also show anger with body language. When bottlenose dolphins swarm together and circle, leap, and slap the water, they are sending a message. They are saying, "We mean business!" They are saying, "Back off!"

Great white sharks are big and tough. They can grow up to 20 feet (4.6 m) long and weigh 5,000 pounds (2,268 kg) or more. Bottlenose dolphins are smaller. They can be 14 feet long (4.2 m) and weigh 1,100 pounds (500 kg). But a great white knows a group of angry dolphins can do serious damage. To protect themselves or their young, a group of dolphins may attack and even kill a shark. So even a great white will usually swim away rather than face a pod of angry dolphins.

In Todd's case, the dolphins may have sensed that the shark was a threat to him. Then they acted to protect him. Scientist Rochelle Constantine of the University of Auckland in New Zealand also studies dolphins. She says, "Dolphins are known for helping helpless things." There's no doubt that Todd Endris was helpless after being attacked by the great white. To Todd, there's no doubt that the heroic dolphins saved his life.

Perched on climbing ropes, gorilla hero Binti Jua looks lost in thought.

BINTI JUA AND JAMBO: GORILLA GOOD GUYS

Binti Jua cradles
her adorable
baby, Koola.

Chapter 1

BOY MEETS GORILLA

It happened quickly, in less than half an hour. But for the parents of one little boy, those minutes felt like forever.

It was August 16, 1996. The mother and father had taken their son to the Brookfield Zoo near Chicago, Illinois. He was three years old. In the afternoon, the family went to see the gorillas. Seven gorillas were in the exhibit that day.

Binti Jua (sounds like BEN-tee WAH) was one of the females. She had a baby named Koola. Koola was 17 months old.

Have you ever seen a gorilla mother and baby together? They are so much fun to watch. Babies tug and tumble. They climb on their moms like jungle gyms. Then, quick as a wink, they cuddle and smooch. Gorilla mothers hug and kiss their babies. The babies hug right back. When they aren't playing or cuddling, gorilla babies ride on their mom's back.

Koola was so cute, she always drew big crowds. Everyone loved to visit her, especially kids. It was exciting.

That afternoon, the three-year-old boy got a little too excited. At one point, his mother looked away. It was only for a moment, but that was all it took. The small boy in a bright red shirt scrambled over the railing. Then, *THUNK*. He fell 18 feet (5.5 m)—almost two stories—down into the gorilla enclosure (sounds like in-KLOH-zhur). When he hit the concrete floor, he was knocked out. He lay there limp as a rag doll.

People gasped in horror. Everyone watching was afraid. No one knew what would happen next. No one knew just how to help. Someone ran to tell the zookeepers what had happened.

The little boy was in terrible danger. Gorillas may be fun to watch, but they are big and they are strong. They don't like surprises like tumbling little boys. Surprises sometimes make gorillas cranky.

Playtime

A newborn gorilla clings to its mother's chest for the first few months of life. Later, it learns to ride on her back. When gorillas turn three, they're ready for fun! Between the ages of three and six, gorillas act a lot like human children do. They spend most of their time playing. They climb trees and swing from branches. They wrestle and tumble. They chase each other round and round and scream with laughter. Sound like anyone you know?

People screamed in fear when one of the gorillas slowly walked toward the child. It was Binti Jua. Little Koola clung to her back.

A paramedic (sounds like pare-uh-MED-ik) named Bill Lambert was watching the gorillas, too. He was there when the boy fell. He even had his video camera rolling. Bill wanted to help the boy. He'd been trained to help in emergencies. But he couldn't reach the child. So he kept filming. He didn't know what to expect. What he captured was an amazing surprise.

It soon became clear that Binti Jua, called Binti for short, didn't want to hurt the boy. She wanted to help him.

Binti scooped up the child's small, still body in her big, furry arms. She carried him across a stream in the gorilla pen. Then she lifted him over a giant log. Binti headed to the zookeeper door at the back of the pen. When she got there, she cradled the boy in her right arm. Koola peeked at the boy from her spot on her mother's back. It was the tiny gorilla's turn to be curious.

The other gorillas also were curious about the boy. One of them growled at him. But Binti Jua wouldn't let the others get close to the child. She rocked him gently. She waited for help to arrive.

Craig Demitros was one of the gorilla experts at the zoo. He was eating lunch when his walkie-talkie went off. Signal 13—an emergency in the gorilla enclosure!

No one had ever fallen in there before, so Craig was surprised. But he knew what to do. He ordered three zookeepers to drive the gorillas into their rooms behind the pen. The zookeepers sprayed streams of water toward the gorillas. This didn't hurt them, but it did help them know which way to go. It also kept them away from Binti Jua and the boy.

Once the other gorillas left the pen, Binti Jua put the boy down. She was very careful with him. Then she followed the other gorillas into the back rooms. Koola still rode on her back.

Now the paramedics could do their job. They rushed the boy to the hospital.

Start to finish, the rescue took only 19 minutes. How did it go so well? The answer is practice, according to Craig. "Our team has safety walks through the enclosures to prepare for emergencies," he says. They'd practiced just a few days before the boy fell.

Being knocked out, or unconscious (sounds like un-CON-shus), also helped the boy. "Because he wasn't crying or screaming, he didn't seem to pose a threat," Craig says. "He also landed on his bottom, not his head. That may have saved his life."

Besides hurting his head, the little boy also had a broken hand. He spent three days in the hospital. Then the doctors said he was well enough to go home. But his parents never revealed his name. They did not want anyone to know who their son was.

For Binti Jua, it was the opposite. People everywhere learned her name. She became a star! Her heroic deed made headlines around the world. TV and radio programs around the world also featured her story.

The Brookfield Zoo's mailbox soon overflowed with letters about Binti Jua. "Congratulations with all our hearts," one group of kids wrote. Lots of kids wrote wanting to know more about her.

Binti even got fancy gifts. One gift was a sparkly, heart-shaped necklace. "Mother of the Year," it said.

Binti Jua munches on one of her favorite snacks. Do you think she knows she's famous?

Chapter 2

BRINGING UP BINTI

Everyone agrees that Binti Jua is a hero. But people still wonder why she did what she did. Why did she help the little boy? Curiosity is one theory (sounds like THEER-ee). Craig at the Brookfield Zoo says, "We think she was closest to where the boy actually fell in." So maybe Binti just wanted to check things out.

Or maybe she wanted to trade the boy—for a snack! Sometimes people drop things into the gorilla cage, like cameras and sunglasses. *Oops!* If the gorillas eat these things, it can make them very sick. So the zookeepers have trained the gorillas to bring things that fall into their cage to the zookeeper's door. As a reward, the apes get a yummy food treat. Maybe that's what Binti was hoping for. Maybe that's why she took the child to the door.

Craig says there could be another reason Binti was so gentle with the boy. It may have to do with the way she grew up.

Binti Jua was born in 1988 at the Columbus Zoo in Ohio. Her mother was a gorilla named Lulu. Her father's name was Sunshine. Binti was named after her father.

In the African language called Swahili (sounds like swah-HEE-lee), Binti Jua means "Daughter of Sunshine."

Lulu couldn't make enough milk to feed Binti. The zookeepers were afraid the baby wouldn't survive. So when Binti was three months old, they sent her to the San Francisco Zoo in California. Now she would be raised by humans.

For the rest of her first year, Binti lived with people, not gorillas. Human caretakers held her. Humans fed her. They played with her. They even slept with her. They were with her 24/7, just like a gorilla mother would be. According to the experts at the San Francisco Zoo, Binti Jua grew up feeling safe with humans. Maybe that's why she wasn't scared of the little boy.

As a baby, Binti even played with a little girl. The girl's name was Jennifer. Her mother worked at the zoo. When the two "kids" met, they reached their hands out to touch each other. It was like they were both human children. It was like they were both gorilla babies, too.

After her first birthday, Binti joined the rest of the gorillas at the San Francisco Zoo. It should have been a good thing. But Binti was sad and lonely. She was younger than the others. She didn't really know how to act around them. She bit a little too hard when she played. And she didn't stop playing when the grown-up gorillas got mad. She just didn't fit in. So the zookeepers decided to find her a new home.

Family Fame

Binti Jua isn't the only famous gorilla in her family. Her Aunt Koko is also a star. Koko lives at the Gorilla Foundation in Woodside, California. Her brother is Binti's father, Sunshine. What makes Koko the gorilla famous? She knows how to communicate using American Sign Language. Scientist Penny Patterson taught her how. Penny showed Koko the video of Binti saving the little boy. Then Penny asked her about Binti. Koko signed "lip"—that's her word for *girl*—and "good." In other words, Koko said Binti was a "good girl"!

When she was three years old, Binti moved to the Brookfield Zoo in Illinois. Everyone hoped it would be a better place for her.

Two other three-year-old gorillas lived at the Brookfield Zoo. The zookeepers hoped they would teach Binti Jua how to behave. It wasn't easy. "It was a school of hard knocks," Craig says. He means that Binti had to learn the hard way. She would scream and run. The other two little gorillas would slap and bite. Scream! Run! Slap! Bite! Binti took her lumps. Finally, she figured out how to act around the others. She learned good gorilla manners. Once she did, Binti was truly at home.

When Binti was six, zookeepers learned that she was expecting her first baby. They were excited. They were also a little worried. Binti had learned how to get along with other gorillas. But would she know how to be a gorilla mom? The zookeepers weren't sure.

Newborn gorillas are helpless and tiny. They weigh only about four pounds (2 kg) at birth. They need a lot of care from their mothers. Gorillas learn how to be mothers from their own mothers. But Binti wasn't raised by her mother, Lulu. She was raised by people. So she had to go to gorilla mommy school.

The zookeepers used a furry stuffed animal to train Binti to be a good mom. They wanted her to learn to carry her baby constantly. So they rewarded her with a treat every time she picked up the toy baby.

If she put it down, no treat. Binti soon learned to hold the stuffed animal all the time. The zookeepers showed her how to cradle it. They even taught her how to feed a baby.

Did You Know?

Gorillas live to be about 35 years old in the wild. In zoos they may live to be more than 50.

Binti gave birth to Koola in February 1995. What kind of mom was she? "She was better than we expected," Craig says. "She was a great mom." The fact that Binti was such a good mother might have led her to protect the human child.

Scientist Penny Patterson is the director of the Gorilla Foundation in Woodside, California. She's also thought about why Binti helped the little boy. Binti might have picked up the boy because it was the motherly thing to do. Female gorillas have been known to show caring and helping behaviors. But Penny says it was Binti's intelligence that told her to bring him to the zookeeper door.

Binti Jua still lives at the Brookfield Zoo. She has never had to rescue another human. But she has had more babies. She's been a super mom to them all. And now Binti's a grandmother! Her daughter Koola has a baby of her own. Koola is a terrific mom, too. But that's not a surprise. She learned from the best—Binti Jua.

Full-grown male gorillas, like this one, are called silverbacks. Jambo was a silverback.

Chapter 3

ANOTHER GREAT APE

Binti Jua amazed people everywhere when she cared for the hurt little boy in 1996. She wasn't the first gorilla to be a worldwide hero, though. She wasn't even the first gorilla to guard a human child. Another gorilla did the same thing ten years earlier. This one wasn't a female. It was a big, bold male gorilla named Jambo (sounds like YAM-bo).

Jambo lived at the Durrell Wildlife Park on Jersey, an island off the coast of England. He was a silverback. That's what full-grown male gorillas are called. They get the name from the silver-colored hair on their lower back.

In the wild, a silverback often acts as the leader of a gorilla group, or troop. He guards the troop. He lets the other gorillas know when it's time to feed or travel or sleep.

Sometimes a silverback shows off by hooting. He stands up and beats his chest. He does this when he feels challenged or threatened. When a gorilla acts like this, it can look scary. But gorillas are usually calm and peaceful—unless something disturbs them, that is. And on August 31, 1986, something very disturbing happened.

That day five-year-old Levan Merrit visited the Durrell Wildlife Park. He went with his parents, Steve and Pauline. His brother, Lloyd, and sister, Stephanie, went, too. The family decided to go see the gorillas. When they got there, however, the kids couldn't see anything. A tall wall surrounded the enclosure. The gorillas were hanging out at the bottom of it. It was hard to see them without leaning over the wall. But the wall was too tall for Levan to lean over.

So Levan's father lifted him on top of the wall for a better look. Then he turned to lift Lloyd up, too. That's when Levan decided to stand up. Bad idea! In an instant, he was falling. Steve heard his son scream, but it was too late to catch him. Levan tumbled into the gorilla pen.

Steve's heart pounded with fear. He looked down and saw his son. Levan lay silent at the bottom of the wall. Steve had to try to save him. He started to climb into the pen with Levan. But people stopped him.

"There was blood all over the place," Steve says, "and I couldn't get to him. I thought he was going to be torn to pieces."

Jambo and the other gorillas were frightened by the tiny stranger in their space. So they scattered. They sounded a warning cry. They hooped and hollered. They screamed. Nandi, a female with gorilla babies of her own, approached the boy. Jambo turned her away. He was probably trying to protect her.

What Jambo did next surprised everyone. Brian LeLion got it all on videotape. Jambo approached the boy slowly. He was trying to figure the boy out. Was Levan a threat to his troop?

The silverback looked the boy over. Then he looked up at the crowd above. It was like Jambo was saying, *What is he doing here?*

Experts say it was a good thing Levan wasn't crying. If so, Jambo might have seen him as a threat. But because Levan was quiet, the silverback stayed close. Other gorillas tried to approach the boy. Jambo waved them off.

Kids Can Help

Binti Jua and Jambo protected human children from harm. You can help protect their relatives living in the wild. Here's how:

- Organize a penny drive. Set up jars or cans at school. Ask people to donate pennies. Send the money to a gorilla rescue group.

- Sponsor a baby gorilla! Families or classrooms can donate money to help care for a baby gorilla at the GRACE Center for Rescued Gorillas (http://gorillafund.org).

- Learn about gorilla protection projects at http://animals.nationalgeographic.com/animals/great-apes/.

- Visit your local zoo. Your admission fee helps gorillas, too.

The human crowd looked on in fear. Someone suggested throwing stones to keep the gorillas away from the boy. But a wise person said no. Throwing rocks might upset the gorillas. Staying calm was the best thing the crowd could do for Levan. Because all the people stayed calm, Jambo did, too. The silverback started to gently pat the boy on the back.

Scientist Penny Patterson of the Gorilla Foundation says Jambo was protecting Levan. She says it's not unusual for male gorillas to show this kind of guarding behavior.

Levan was unconscious for ten minutes. Jambo guarded him the whole time. Then all of a sudden the quiet ended. Levan woke up and started to cry. This alarmed

Jambo. The silverback left the little boy. He ran back to the indoor area at the back of the enclosure. The zookeepers had already gathered most of the other gorillas indoors.

One younger male gorilla refused to go inside. His name was Hobbit. He was curious. He ignored the keepers. He darted down to where Levan was crying. What would Hobbit do next? No one knew. It was time for action.

Firefighters were on the scene by now. They lowered paramedic Brian Fox into the gorilla enclosure. "The boy was bleeding and in pain," Brian said. "It was my job to get in the pen and help Levan out."

The zookeepers joined Brian in the pen. They held large sticks. As Hobbit came close, they stood tall. They waved their sticks in the air. They were not trying to hurt Hobbit. Hobbit probably wasn't trying to hurt them, either. They just wanted to scare him away. They wanted to keep everyone safe, gorillas and humans. It worked.

Brian started to treat the cut on the back of Levan's head. But he was afraid the little boy was very badly hurt. There was no time to waste.

The firefighters tossed Brian a rope. He tied it around his body. Then he scooped up Levan. The firefighters pulled and pulled on the rope. They lifted Brian and Levan out of the pen. Then they rushed Levan to the hospital. Levan was very lucky. He would be fine.

The video of the rescue thrilled viewers around the world. People called Jambo a hero. They called him the Gentle Giant. More people came to the zoo to see Jambo. Scientists wanted to study him.

Jambo showed the world a new, gentle side to the giant apes. Binti Jua did, too. Thanks to these gorilla "good guys," two curious little boys lived to see another day.

THE END

DON'T MISS!

NATIONAL GEOGRAPHIC KiDS **CHAPTERS**

BEST FRIENDS FOREVER!

And More True Stories of Animal Friendships

By Amy Shields

Turn the page
for a sneak preview . . .

Bubbles gives a
lift to Suryia,
Roscoe, and
animal trainer
Moksha Bybee.

Chapter 1

The BEST DAY Ever

Summer 2008,
Myrtle Beach, South Carolina

It was a muggy, hot day. An elephant named Bubbles strolled through the woods. On her back bounced a fuzzy-haired orangutan named Suryia (sounds like SUR-ee-uh). Bubbles and Suryia were excited. They knew there was a river at the end of the path. Soon they were going to be *in* that river. They were going for a swim!

A man named Doc walked beside Bubbles and Suryia. Looking ahead, he saw a hound dog. It sat alone on the riverbank. It looked like a hungry dog. It was so skinny you could see its ribs. Just then, Suryia spied the dog, too. Before Doc could stop him, the playful ape jumped off Bubbles.

Suryia ran to the dog. He threw his long, hairy arms around it. *Uh-oh,* thought Doc. *A hungry dog might be a mean dog.*

But the dog didn't mind a big, hairy hug. He even wagged his tail. Then he pounced at Suryia. The seven-year-old orangutan pounced back. That was their I-like-you, do-you-like-me? moment. The answer was yes!

The new pals chased each other in circles. Then they flopped down to rest. The orangutan put his arm around the dog. He pulled him close. They acted "like long lost friends," Doc said.

After a while it was time to leave. Doc lifted Suryia back onto Bubbles. He tried to send the dog back to its own home.

But the dog followed them. He wagged his tail all the way. Wherever Suryia was, that's where the dog wanted to be. "I guess you've decided to stay," said Doc. He named the dog Roscoe.

Doc is Dr. Bhagavan Antle (sounds like BAG-uh-vahn ANN-tuhl). He is the director of a wildlife preserve in Myrtle Beach, South Carolina. Suryia and Bubbles are just two of the animals that live there.

Doc and the other caregivers at the preserve also look after lions and tigers. They care for leopards and cheetahs. They watch over monkeys, chimpanzees, and other orangutans like Suryia. There's even a liger (sounds like LIE-ger) named Hercules at the preserve. A liger is the cub of a lion father and a tiger mother.

Now Doc had a new animal to take care of, and Suryia had a new best friend.

Roscoe is a bluetick coonhound. Blueticks are smart and friendly. They really like to hunt. Blueticks keep their noses to the ground, sniffing for clues. They forget everything except *Find it, find it!*

Island Homes

Orangutans used to live everywhere in Asia. Today they live in the wild on only two small islands. These are Sumatra (sounds like sue-MAH-tra) and Borneo (sounds like BORE-nee-oh).

Wild orangutans make their homes in rain forests. Farmers and loggers are cutting down the forests on these islands. They want to make palm tree farms. This leaves orangutans with even fewer places to live. It is harder for them to find food. Unless their forest homes are protected, there will soon be no more wild orangutans.

A bluetick coonhound won't stop until it catches its prey or chases it up a tree.

Roscoe might have been hunting the day he met Suryia. Maybe he went too far. Maybe he could not find his way back home. Maybe he did not have a home.

At first, Doc kept a careful eye on Suryia and Roscoe. Animals often get scared when something new enters their world. Suryia had never been face-to-face with a dog before. Had Roscoe ever met an orangutan? Not likely!

Scared dogs growl. They show their teeth. Their ears go back. The hair on their back stands straight up. When orangutans get scared, they look like they're smiling. A silly grin on their face means they're shaking inside. Doc never saw anything like that on Suryia's face. And Roscoe never growled. He never showed other signs of fear, either. Not even once.

Since the day they met, it's been Suryia and Roscoe, best friends forever. Neither one is the boss. If Roscoe wants to nap, Suryia flops down beside him. If Suryia lies down to rest, Roscoe does, too.

Suryia is better at sharing than Roscoe, however. Suryia shares everything. He breaks up his cookies and feeds pieces to Roscoe. Roscoe really likes Suryia's special monkey cookies.

Suryia also tries to share bananas with Roscoe. Roscoe does *not* like bananas. He will not open his mouth. He turns his face away. Then Suryia gives up...

Want to know what happens next? Be sure to check out *Best Friends Forever!* Available wherever books and ebooks are sold.

INDEX

Boldface indicates illustrations.

Binti Jua (gorilla) **68–69, 70, 80**
    motherhood 86–88, 89
    raised by humans 80–89
    rescue of boy 70–79, 88–89
Bottlenose dolphins **36–37, 48**
    communications 52, **52,** 66
    echolocation 63, **63**
    protecting surfer 42, 46–47,
        61, 64–67
    protecting swimmers 49,
        53–57

Connor, Richard 65–66
Constantine, Rochelle 67
Cooper, Karina 50–51, 53–57

Demitros, Craig 76–78, 81–82, 86
Dogs, wild 32, **32**

Endris, Todd
    dolphin heroes 42, 46–47, 61,
        64, 67
    rescue and recovery 59–62
    shark attack 44–47, 64
    surfing **38,** 39–42, 44, **58**

Fennec fox 32, **32**
Fleet, Matt 55–57
Fox, Brian 98–100

Gorillas 74, **74, 90,** 96
Great white sharks **43**
    attacking surfer 41–42, 44–
        47, 59, 62, 64, 67
    attacking swimmers 55–57
    eating people 43

Hobbit (gorilla) 98–99
Howe, Nicole 49–51, 53–57
Howe, Rob 49–51, 53–57

Jambo (gorilla) 90–100
Jansen, Joe 47

Klimley, A. Peter 43
Koko (gorilla) 85, **85**
Koola (gorilla) **70,** 72, 75, 76, 77,
    88, 89

Lambert, Bill 75
Lanteigne, David
    adopting Lilly 8–12, 14–15
    Lilly's injury 20–22, 24–25
    Lilly's new career 27–28, 31,
        33–35
LeLion, Brian 95
Lilly (pit bull) **4–5, 6, 16**
    adopted by David 6–12, 14–15
    injury and recovery 19–22,
        24–25, **26,** 27–31
    rescuing Christine 16–25
    showing pit bull nature 33–35

Merrit, Levan 93–95, 97–100

Nandi (gorilla) 94–95

Patterson, Penny 85, **85,**
    88–89, 97
Penny (dog) 11, 14, **16,** 17
Pit bulls 13, **13,** 14–15, 23, **23**

Simpson, Brian 44, 60
Slade, Helen 50–51, 53–57

Williams, Wes 47

MORE INFORMATION

To find more information about the animal species featured in this book, check out these books and websites:

Dolphins, by Melissa Stewart, National Geographic, 2010

Face to Face With Gorillas, by Michael Nichols, National Geographic, 2009

Saving Audie: A Pit Bull Puppy Gets a Second Chance, by Dorothy Hinshaw Patent, Walker Children's, 2011

Bad Rap Pit Bull Rescue
www.badrap.org

Dian Fossey Gorilla Fund
http://gorillafund.org

The Gorilla Foundation
http://koko.org/foundation

Lilly the Hero Pit Bull
http://lillytheheropitbull.com

National Geographic, "Animals: Bottlenose Dolphins,"
http://animals.nationalgeographic.com/animals/mammals/bottlenose-dolphin

This book is dedicated to heroic animals and the people who sometimes rescue them all over the world. May we live up to their examples.
—K.M.H.

CREDITS

Thanks to the National Geographic Channel for the photo of Todd Endris on page 38, as seen in Nat Geo WILD's *Shark Attack Experiment: LIVE!*

Cover, Lindsay Dancy - LDancy Design and Co-founder of Lilly Fund Boston, MA; 4-5, © David R. Lanteigne; 6, © David R. Lanteigne; 13, Courtesy of Animal Farm Foundation; 16 (up), © David R. Lanteigne; 16 (lo), © David R. Lanteigne; 23, National World War I Museum Archives, Kansas City, Missouri; 26, © David R. Lanteigne; 32, Dbajurin/Dreamstime.com; 36-37, Dray van Beeck/Shutterstock; 38, Courtesy of Todd Endris; 43, Sandra Lucas/Dreamstime.com; 48, Anteromite/Shutterstock; 52, Croisy/Shutterstock; 58, George Nikitin, PacificCoastNews/Newscom; 63, Willyam Bradberry/Shutterstock; 68-69, Jim Schulz/Chicago Zoological Society; 70, Jim Schulz/Chicago Zoological Society; 74, Petra Wegner/Alamy; 80, JimSchulz/Chicago Zoological Society; 85, Ron Cohn/Gorilla Foundation/koko.org; 90, © Brian Le Lion; 96, Mike Price/Shutterstock; 101, Stevi Calandra/National Geographic Channels; 102, MyrtleBeachSafari.com/Barry Bland; 107, Stephaniellen/Shutterstock; 111, © Beth Oram 2012.

ACKNOWLEDGMENTS

These stories could not have been told without the help of Lilly's owner, Officer David R. Lanteigne; the gorilla keeper at the Brookfield Zoo, Craig Demitros; and other generous experts.